THE GIFTS OF CHRISTMAS

THE GIFTS OF CHRISTMAS

by RACHEL HARTMAN
Illustrated by John Alcorn

PUBLISHED BY CHANNEL PRESS, INC., MANHASSET, N. Y.

THE GIFTS OF CHRISTMAS

Text copyright © 1962 by Rachel Hartman
Illustrations copyright © 1962 by Channel Press, Inc.

LIBRARY OF CONGRESS CATALOG CARD NUMBER:
62-18045
MANUFACTURED IN THE UNITED STATES OF AMERICA

CONTENTS

The Gift of the Shepherds:
WONDER 7

The Gift of Mary and Joseph:
LOVING PREPARATION 17

The Gift of The Father:
THE LIGHT OF THE WORLD 35

The Gift of The Baby:
JOY 49

The Gift of the Angels:
MUSIC 63

The Gift of the Nations:
REMEMBRANCE 85

The Gift of the Wise Men:
THEIR BEST 107

THE GIFT OF THE SHEPHERDS
WONDER

AMONG THE VERY FIRST PERSONS TO SEE THE INFANT
Jesus were the shepherds who brought to the Christ
Child a very precious gift—the gift of wonder.

The shepherds were simple, uneducated men, their
minds and hands occupied with the constant tasks of
finding green pastures, of keeping wild animals from

preying on their flocks, of providing food and clothing for their own families. But on the hillside just outside Bethlehem that dark night their lives were touched in a special way, and they responded quickly to the message of the angel.

It is recorded in Luke that "the glory of the Lord" had shone around the shepherds, and that "they were sore afraid" until they heard the reassuring words of the angel, "Fear not: for behold I bring you good tidings of great joy . . . for unto you is born . . . a Saviour which is Christ the Lord."

These shepherds were watchful, careful, conscientious men, as all good shepherds must be. They were occupied with their daily tasks, but they were not preoccupied with temporal things, for when they heard the angel's words they also saw a great light, and wonder touched their hearts and minds. They said to one another, "Let us go even unto Bethlehem, and see this thing which is come to pass." They arose and went, bearing the gift of wonder in their hearts and eyes.

Suppose we had been on that hillside that dark night? Might we not have talked ourselves out of the journey while walking to town? Or if we had arrived in Bethlehem, might we not then have decided that the heavenly visitation was an illusion? But the shepherds persisted until they found that which they had been told they would see: a "babe, wrapped in swaddling clothes and lying in a manger."

Artists' interpretations sometimes show the shepherds presenting a lamb to the Christ Child. It is possible that one of these country men carried a lamb in his arms, and placed it at the manger-bed; but it is just as probable that the shepherds had left the hillside in such haste that they had no time to think of a gift for the Child out of their frugal means and possessions. The gift they *did* bring, however, was priceless. They brought wonder, belief. They came in simplicity of spirit and with wonder in their hearts, even as you and I can come today.

The shepherds, no doubt, were familiar with the prophecy from their Scriptures of the promise of the One who would be called "Counselor, the mighty God, the everlasting Father, the Prince of Peace" (*Isaiah 9:6*). Their hearts had been somewhat prepared, and so they believed the angel's words that this Babe in swaddling clothes was the "Saviour which is Christ the Lord." Some scholars give expression to the thought that these shepherds truly worshipped Jesus, while the Wise Men, pagans from lands of superstition, only paid homage to a child who they thought would one day be King of Israel.

Because the Magi came with gifts in their hand and travelled so far, and because they journeyed from the East wearing fine raiment and jewels, we may think them more important than the rough-clad shepherds who came empty-handed to the manger, travelling only

9

a few short miles from the hillside outside Bethlehem. But the shepherds had come "with haste," and they were men who believed that a miracle *could* happen close by, in their own home town. They were quick of foot and equally quick of heart. Their hands, perhaps, were empty, but their hearts were full of wonder. This was their gift to the Christ Child, and to us.

After their visit to the manger, touched by their experience, they went about Bethlehem spreading the news, repeating to others the message the angel had given them, and telling that they had seen confirmation of it in the stable. They were the first proclaimers of the good news. They had seen the Child born in a manger. Their words aroused curiosity among the people. Some believed. Others doubted, even as today. But it is recorded in Luke that all who heard it "wondered at those things which were told them by the shepherds." The people "who had ears to hear" caught the spirit of wonder.

Can we picture the shepherds talking of their experiences, their eyes shining, their tongues filled with praise? Perhaps they used the familiar words of one of their psalms, "O come, let us worship and bow down: let us kneel before the Lord our maker" (*Psalm 95:6*), a thought re-echoed today in one of our best-known Christmas hymns, "O come, let us adore Him."

Perhaps on their way back to the hillside they sang another psalm, "Blessed be the Lord God, the God of

Israel, who only doeth wondrous things. And blessed be His glorious name forever: and let the whole earth be filled with His glory; Amen, and Amen" (*Psalm 72:18, 19*). The shepherds must have returned to their simple, prosaic tasks in new spirit, for it is written that "they glorified and praised God." They had been touched with a continuing radiance of wonder. They had been to Bethlehem, the beginning of Christmas.

So, in like spirit, today "let *us* go even unto Bethlehem. . . ."

This book is intended to mark out a spiritual journey for those who would see the Christ Child clearly through the haze and confusion cast on this happiest of our holidays by tradition, legend, commercialization and custom. This will be a journey for individuals and, we hope, for families. There will be suggestions to help make Christmas meaningful and enjoyable for the youngster as well as the adult. We will be able to look behind many of our holiday customs to see their source and their spiritual significance.

If we, today, journey to Bethlehem in spirit as the shepherds did so long ago, with wonder in our hearts, then we should take time for preparation and meditation.

We need to shut out the demands and noises of the everyday, for if all is rush and tension at this season of the year, we shall miss the meaning of Christmas, the reason for keeping this day set apart. We need to establish a place and time for quiet, to prepare our hearts for Christmas and to nurture the spirit of wonder.

For some, this spirit of wonder will be most evident while meditating reverently in a hushed church. Others will catch the radiance while listening to exalting music. Still others will discover it while walking under starlight, feeling kinship with the shepherds on that night when the angels appeared.

Special services, held in churches during Advent and the Christmas season, help to prepare our hearts and minds, and, indeed, at no time are our churches more beautiful. The very name, "Christmas," comes from a church service. The tradition of the Christmas Eve midnight service has been a highlight of the year in Roman Catholic churches. In Protestant churches, too, the Christmas Eve service is growing in importance, and is usually a quiet, meditative service with beautiful music, a time of high devotion.

But the Christmas season is also a time for worship in the home. A daily period of meditation will help to prepare our hearts for Christmas, individually and as a family. A worship center can add significance to family devotions. This center may be composed of candles flanking a lovely print of the Nativity scene by an old master, or can be a beautiful Poinsettia or other flowering plant, or perhaps an Advent wreath or a creche.

Children sometimes enjoy making tryptichs from old greeting cards, and these are ideal objects for the worship center. Every reminder of the birthday of Jesus placed in the home will help make the holiday season more blessed for children and adults.

When the Christmas story is read to children and they begin to ask such questions as, "Why were the shepherds afraid of the angel?" there is wonderful opportunity to take time to explain the splendor and joy of Christmas. Parents may wish to write down the sweet and significant sayings of their children to treasure in years to come.

Children have the expectant, joyous wonder of Christmas in their minds at this time of year, while adults have the greater joy of watching this wonder grow from week to week and from year to year. Adults may enter the world of wonder vicariously through the eyes of the child, and thus they further increase their own sense of wonder. Take time to help a child experience this emotion. Nothing can replace the joy of watching a child's expression, for instance, while he is lighting a candle during a devotional period in the home. Participation by all will leave its glowing memory for both child and parent.

So, "let *us* go even unto Bethlehem . . ."—preparing our hearts in meaningful ways for Christmas, renewing the spirit of wonder, hope and adoration in our own lives.

When Jesus was born, Joseph and Mary together must have lavished their love and care upon the infant. Certain preparations were made for this birth, as for that of every wanted baby. Mary undoubtedly brought with her to Bethlehem the bands of cloth with which she swaddled the little one. Following the custom of generations, no doubt, the Baby Jesus was washed, rubbed with salt, and laid on a square of cloth which was then folded carefully around Him. Then He was probably wrapped in long narrow cloth strips that held His tiny arms to His sides. These were the swaddling clothes; for several months after their birth, almost all infants of this time were kept in swaddling clothes, designed to give support to their little backs. During the daytime hours the swaddling bands were loosened and the baby's tender skin rubbed with olive oil and dusted with powdered myrtle leaves.

Mary must have used the best knowledge of her time to care for the Baby Jesus. She knew perhaps instinctively that all babies need love. And we can be sure that the tiny Son of God received affection from the very beginning, because both Mary and Joseph were prepared for His coming. When Mary had visited her cousin, Elizabeth, after the angel had appeared unto her making his annunciation, Mary responded in beautiful words which tell us of her preparation of heart for the great event. Probably her thoughts then were influenced by her knowledge of the song of Hannah at the miracu-

What greater gift can we bring today to the Christ Child than our gift of wonder? Wonder—the precious, intangible gift of the shepherds so long ago.

"And it came to pass, as the angels were gone away from them into heaven, the shepherds said one to another, Let us now go even unto Bethlehem, and see this thing which is come to pass, which the Lord hath made known unto us. And they came with haste, and found Mary, and Joseph, and the babe lying in a manger."

—LUKE 2:15, 16

LOVING
PREPARATIO

ONE OF THE MOST TOUCHING INCID
Nativity story is that of Joseph trying
for the weary Mary, and being turned av
sisted until he found the stable. Joseph
with gentleness, we know, for Joseph
remembered as a gentle man.

17

lous birth of Samuel. But Mary's song, called the Magnificat and recorded in *Luke 1:46-48*, is much more beautiful:

My soul doth magnify the Lord,
And my spirit hath rejoiced in God my Saviour.

Mary had prepared her heart for Jesus, though she continued to marvel at the wonder of this unusual Baby and to "ponder these things in her heart." Joseph had received messages in dreams about this child, and so his heart, too, was prepared.

To some people today, getting ready for Christmas is more important than the occasion itself. "Have you finished your shopping?" is a question often heard during the weeks preceding Christmas. Stores rush to display their holiday merchandise in order to take advantage of every possible sale. In some cities, street decorations are rushed out of storage and hung early in November, and carols are noisily broadcast from loudspeakers before the end of that month. This pushing of the season often makes people weary of the thought of Christmas before the date actually arrives, and so the holy day becomes an anticlimax.

In many towns and cities across our country, concerned men and women have pondered this dilemma and have organized committees to help keep alive the religious aspects of Christmas, and to prevent commercial interests from extending the season immoderately. In Cincinnati, for instance, the "Christ in Christmas Committee" was organized in 1951, and has been working effectively ever since. This group secured immediate cooperation from business and civic organizations; stores agreed to wait until after Thanksgiving for Christmas advertising. They also decided to give attention in their window displays to the sacred meaning of the holiday. Their emphasis during the first few years was: "You don't celebrate a birth until the child arrives. December 25 is the birth of Christ, the beginning of Christmas." The consistent work of this committee has affected the entire tone of the city's celebration, and has had its effect on individual and family life as well. Christmas becomes more meaningful to those who remember the true purpose of the season—who plan, simplify and organize their activities, their gift buying, gift wrapping and other tasks so that the weeks before Christmas are a happy bustle rather than a heavy burden.

The traditional period of Christmastide lasts until Twelfth Night, January 6, and so some programs and festivities can and should be held over to the days immediately following Christmas Day. If more churches and organizations delayed their programs and parties until after Christmas, the days of preparation would certainly be more tranquil.

Simplifying our lives at Christmas is a responsibility each of us faces, if we would have time to prepare our spirit. This is a time when parents should share more and not less time with their children. We owe it to those we love to be relaxed and happy, not tired, irritable and jittery.

In many homes, housecleaning and decorating are traditional ways to prepare for the holiday. Women of Scandinavian descent feel the need to scrub the house from top to bottom, as is the custom in the old country. But with modern conveniences, today's homes are kept cleaner year 'round than our grandmothers would have thought possible. Decorating the house for Christmas is more a creative expression and artistic pleasure than a chore, but requires a great deal of time when done on an elaborate scale. Perhaps here, too, we can simplify the work.

In recent years Christmas trees have been set up in some homes so early that needles fall and there is dust on the ornaments by Christmas Day. How sad on December 26 to see dry, discarded evergreens, with silver icicles still clinging to the branches, lying limp alongside the trash can at the curb. And Christmas has only begun!

If we celebrate the holiday as the birth of Christ we will want to prepare beforehand, but our actual celebration will begin on Christmas Day.

The Church has always kept a period of preparation for Christmas, called Advent, which means coming. Advent has four Sundays and always begins on the Sunday nearest November 30. Traditionally this is a time of penitence and heart-preparation, yet it does not have the somber aspects of Lent.

The custom of making the Advent wreath, hung in the home during this season, apparently originated in Germany, but is also found in the Scandinavian countries and is growing in popularity here. Making an Advent wreath is a delightful way for the family to prepare for Christmas. Usually four candles, representing the four centuries of waiting for Christ, are set in a wreath of evergreens, this circle denoting eternity. A holder for the candles may be made by drilling holes in a board, or they may be firmly set in a plaster-of-paris

mold in an old pie pan. In any event, they should be secure. The base can be covered with damp sand to prolong the life of the greens, though undoubtedly these will need to be replaced at least once.

The colors of the candles can vary according to preference. Those who strictly follow the liturgical calendar prefer to use three purple candles and one rose-colored, the latter to be used on the third Sunday in Advent. Others may choose all red, all white or all purple. (Purple is the liturgical color for periods emphasizing penitence; in this case it also indicates royalty, in preparation for the coming of the King.)

On the first Sunday in Advent one candle is lighted, a Scripture passage is read, and there are prayers. Each day of the week this same candle is lit again during the family devotional period. On the second Sunday two candles are lit, and so on. During the final week, all four are ablaze. Children enjoy this progression toward Christmas, and the devotional period becomes increasingly meaningful.

If necessary, new candles can replace those burned down far enough to be dangerous. A variation of this arrangement places a fifth candle in the center—a tall white one—to be lighted on Christmas Day, symbolic of the Christ Child.

In the German custom, a star is added to the wreath each day. (Most German families hang the wreath, but many American families prefer to rest it firmly on a table.) One side of the star contains an Old Testament prophecy of the birth of Jesus, the other side the New Testament fulfillment of the prophecy. The children often memorize the verses. (These may be found in the reference section of your Bible.)

Other Advent customs can heighten anticipation. Small children will enjoy an Advent calendar, which is a beautiful picture with twenty-four windows to open, one each day, thus revealing tiny pictures. It is climaxed by the window that opens on the Nativity scene. Church supply houses and some religious book stores carry Advent calendars.

A special large Advent candle, marked to represent the days of Advent and decorated with Christian symbols, is another device that aids us in preparing our hearts for Christmas. The candle is lighted each day during prayer, and as the candle burns down, children know that Christmas Day is approaching.

Some families prepare a large Star of David from six narrow strips of white paper to use at mealtimes during Advent. On each of the strips is printed one of the prophecies of the coming of Christ. The star is placed in the center of the table and rotated so that each day another member of the family reads a new prophecy. By the end of Advent the whole family will know the verses.

Forcing flowers in the house for Christmas is an old custom which has an element of happy anticipation. On December 4, bring in branches from fruit trees, forsythia bushes and the like, and place them in water in a warm room. The flowers will seem to express their praise and adoration to Christ by bursting into bloom, a symbol of the beauty of all life and especially the life of Christ, the One called "altogether lovely."

A Jesse Tree is yet another interesting way to point out to a child the fact that Jesus was the long-awaited One. The name, Jesse, comes, of course, from the father of David, an illustrious ancestor of Jesus, as recorded in the New Testament (*Matthew 1:6*). This "family tree" can be made from any bare branch, fastened in a holder.

The children can make ornaments for the tree from construction paper, each depicting an event or person in the line of the Messiah, or pointing forward to Him. A sheep could be a reminder of the patriarch Abraham, a ladder could indicate Jacob, tiny tablets the law of Moses, a scroll the prophecy of Isaiah, a crown the reign of David.

From Hungary comes the ancient custom of growing wheat for the Christ Child. Wheat seeds are planted in small flower pots on December 13, kept in a moderately warm room and watered daily. On Christmas Eve the plants are placed near the manger to symbolize the coming of Christ, the "Bread of Life."

There are special hymns for Advent which have great meaning and sense of anticipation. Perhaps the best known is the ancient plainsong, "O Come, O Come, Emmanuel," a twelfth-century hymn translated from the Latin. Charles Wesley's "Come, Thou Long Expected Jesus" is most appropriate at this season, as are "Hail to the Lord's Anointed" and "Watchman, Tell Us of the Night."

Another practice that is growing is the reading of selected passages of Scripture every day between Thanksgiving and Christmas, using the list prepared by the American Bible Society.* This provides both a link with

* Available without charge by mail from American Bible Society, 450 Park Avenue, New York 22, New York.

absent loved ones and a sense of concerted action. Praying each day for six persons outside your family circle, people for whom you have never prayed before, is another way to enrich one's preparation of the heart for Christmas.

A fitting way to ready the heart for God's great gift is to give something of yourself. During this season, visits to older or sick persons are tokens of love appreciated particularly by those shut off from their families in nursing homes or in homes for the aged.

A child who fully participates in preparations for Christmas enjoys the holiday and does not have his thoughts only on what he is going to receive. Adults who open their hearts to the true meaning of the season are able to remember Mary and Joseph in their loving and tender preparations for the coming of the Infant Saviour.

"Sitting" with the children of a young mother or with an aged or handicapped person to free another for shopping or for some special service can bring great joy. Clipping items from newspapers and magazines that you know will be of special interest to a friend is still another way of giving yourself.

Children should be encouraged in this type of giving, and in making gifts for presentation to relatives and friends. One such gift for Mother could be offered in a little old-fashioned shoe or stocking cut from construction paper, doubled and then glued on all edges except

the top. This makes a Christmas tree ornament and may be hung, but the real gift is placed inside on Christmas Eve—a slip of paper on which the child has written a promise of something he will do for his mother, a gift of his time.

Making ornaments for the tree and decorations for the house provides happy pre-Christmas activities for youngsters. If they share in the preparations the holiday will mean all the more to them. They can make artificial snow from detergent and a tiny bit of water, beating it into a stiff fluff with a rotary beater. Dab this on windows, evergreens or anywhere you want a snowy effect, for it washes off easily afterward. Balls of the stuff can be made to hang on the tree if a hanger is inserted before drying, and a sparkly effect can be attained by adding glitter to the soft "snow."

There is no end to the variety of ornaments which can be made with paper and foil. Many children enjoy stringing old-fashioned strands of popcorn to loop on the tree, or they tie on popcorn balls or decorative cookies protected with Saran wrap.

Some families add one new ornament each year which has special meaning to all the family. Together they review the events of the year and select the one most outstanding to all of them. On Christmas Eve they place on the tree an object symbolizing that event, offering a prayer of thanks for all the blessings the family has received during the year. One family might add a souvenir of a memorable vacation, or a tiny model of the new car which has brought so much pleasure; another might add the baby's identification bracelet from the hospital.

To be ready for Christmas we may need to do housecleaning after all—in our hearts. This is a time to clean out the grudges, the bitterness, the negativism, the emotions which would keep us from a happy Nativity season. When the Day arrives, we should be able to sing, *"Oh come to my heart, Lord Jesus. There is room in my heart for Thee."*

"*And it came to pass in those days, that there went out a decree from Caesar Augustus, that all the world should be taxed. . . . And Joseph also went up from Galilee, out of the city of Nazareth, into Judaea, unto the city of David, which is called Bethlehem; (because he was of the house and lineage of David:) To be taxed with Mary his espoused wife, being great with child. And so it was, that, while they were there, the days were accomplished that she should be delivered. And she brought forth her firstborn son, and wrapped him in swaddling clothes, and laid him in a manger; because there was no room for them in the inn.*"

—LUKE 2:1, 4-7.

THE GIFT OF THE FATHER

THE LIGHT OF THE WORLD

THE WHOLE IDEA OF GIFTS BEGAN WITH GOD. IF GOD had not been on the giving hand and mankind had not been the recipient of His great gift of love, we today would never have thought of gift-giving among our families and friends. But God showed us the way to love and good will when He sent His greatest gift to earth, on that first Christmas when Jesus was born.

And although we may not be able to explain the mystery of it all, we can accept God's great gift of love.

"Every good gift and every perfect gift is from above and cometh down from the Father of lights" (*James 1:17*). It is most appropriate that this gift from the Father of lights—His Son—should be called the Light of the World. The coming of Jesus to earth means that God is revealed to us through Jesus, the Light of the World.

This miracle of the Incarnation—God becoming man —is one which sages and saints have tried to explain through the ages. They have helped us to understand and to accept this gift, and yet there remains a blessed mystery which no man can quite explain. Even the Apostle Paul, with his great gift of expression, could not explain it. But he did *accept* it: "Thanks be unto God for his unspeakable gift," he said (*II Corinthians 9:15*).

The priest Zacharias, who was the father of John the Baptist, recognized the coming of Jesus as a sunrise, "the dayspring from on high . . . , To give light to them that sit in darkness and in the shadow of death, to guide our feet into the way of peace" (*Luke 1:78, 79*).

Long before Jesus' birth the prophet Isaiah had spoken of that "dawn," too. "The people that walked in darkness have seen a great light: they that dwell in the land of the shadow of death, upon them hath the light shined" (*Isaiah 9:2*).

But perhaps many of us today can best explain this gift, as they did long ago with the name Emmanuel, which means "God with us." In the birth of Jesus, the Light of the World, God *is* with us. It is a glorious thought, and about as close as most of us will get to understanding the theology of it. But even so, we can rejoice that God sent a baby to reveal His love and mercy to us. And we can keep alive the true meaning of Christmas in our customs, our practices, by remembering the past, and by renewing our spirits, just as others have done before us while cherishing the true meaning of Christmas.

In the year 1223 a gentle-spirited Italian monk by the name of Francis longed for a way to make Christmas more meaningful to his parishioners. He decided to try to make the Nativity story come alive, so that these simple people would understand the coming of the Saviour. Bethlehem, the angels, the star, the manger— it had all happened so long ago that these people perhaps believed it was only a beautiful, fanciful tale or "legend." Francis wanted them to visualize the scene at the stable, to understand the gift of God. So he set up a living Nativity scene at the church in Greccio, near Assisi. There in the manger bed of straw was the Baby, with Mary and Joseph nearby.

People flocked to church for this unusual sort of

"preaching." The message got through to them; the birth of Christ became a reality, no longer only the words of a story told by a monk. Francis repeated the living Christmas scene the following year and then the next, until the idea caught the imagination of priests and people of other parishes. Eventually it spread over Europe. Soon every church had a Christmas scene and drama, and still the custom grew. The only fault was that soon one parish tried to outdo another. The living crèches became so elaborate that sometimes the Baby, Mary and Joseph were relegated to incidental positions; even in medieval times the Church was concerned with the secularization of Christmas!

Today the presentation of Nativity scenes with quite realistic mannequins is a Christmas custom in many American cities. Sometimes people actually pose in the tableau, changing the cast in twenty-minute relays.

Some communities also sponsor elaborate Nativity pageants. One of the oldest in America, held in Bethlehem, Pennsylvania, has been less publicized in recent years because of congested traffic and the large crowds that attend, people coming from many miles away.

This industrial city in Pennsylvania's rich farm country is an interesting place at the Christmas season because of its Moravian heritage and because its founding, more than 200 years ago, is linked with this holiday. Sometimes it is called "the Christmas town." The tiny settlement in Pennsylvania had just been formed when

Count Nicholas von Zinzendorf, leader of the Moravians, arrived from Europe on December 24, 1741. The people gathered for a Christmas service in the one log cabin that had been completed and the Count's daughter led them in the singing of a Christmas hymn. Then, carrying a lighted candle, Count Zinzendorf led a procession, all the people following him into the adjoining stable, reminiscent of the scene in Bethlehem. When the hymn was finished he said solemnly, "In memory of the Christ Child let this place be called Bethlehem."

And Bethlehem it is to this day. Each year on December 4 a large star is lighted high on South Mountain, and a public service is held in Zinzendorf Square. Churches in town still observe many of the ancient Christmas customs which their founders brought from their native Moravia.

This Pennsylvania Dutch country is also famous for a custom similar to one that is a tradition in many modern homes and churches today. It is called the *putz*, an elaboration of the miniature Nativity scene known also in other countries; the French call it a *crèche*, the Germans a crib, the Italians *praesepe*. Along with the figures of Mary, Joseph and the Baby in the stable, the *putz* shows an entire landscape—hills and valleys, farmyards, villages with people going about their work, and the Wise Men on camels making their way toward the stable in Bethlehem. Sometimes these scenes are set in gardens, with the figures placed on a bed of moss, and with various plants serving as trees. These miniatures, like the pageant and tableau, trace their origin to the scene St. Francis devised so long ago in the little town of Greccio.

Today the crèche is a tradition in many American homes at Christmastime, no matter what the national background. Figurines wrapped in family memories are lovingly unpacked and set up year after year. Perhaps the children are especially careful with the lamb with the broken ear, remembering the time the cat pulled it off the table. Some crèche figures no doubt are valuable antiques, beautifully carved or molded; others may be made of simple plaster, cast and painted by the children, but are just as beloved because of memories. There may be straw angels from Scandinavia, olive-wood camels from Jordan, pottery figures from South America among the objects, or delicately carved wooden figures from the home workshops of Bavarian woodcarvers, such as the Lang family of Oberammergau (almost as famous for their hand carvings as for their part in the famous Passion Play).

If, in preparing the creche in our homes, the European custom is followed strictly, the miniature manger is left empty until Christmas Eve or Christmas morning—and then the figure of the Christ Child is placed in it by some member of the family. The Wise Men in the meantime have been moved along in their journey a little closer to the manger each day, finally reaching the Bethlehem spot on Twelfth Night, the traditional day for celebrating the adoration of the Magi.

Another important symbol of our Christmastide is the star symbolizing the one the Wise Men followed. We find stars lighting our Christmas decorations and our Christmas trees—usually the five-pointed "star of Bethlehem," occasionally the six-pointed "star of David."

Star decorations have their important place and are lighted in many cities. Roanoke, Virginia, which calls itself the "star city of the South," has a 100-foot star atop Mill Mountain, within the city limits, which was first lighted on a Christmas Eve. During the season the star glows red instead of its usual white.

Lighted stars appear in windows of homes and are

hung across streets in business sections all over the country. Whenever we see them we should be reminded not only of the light which led the Wise Men, but also of God's wonderful Gift called "the bright and morning star."

Light plays a prominent part in the celebration to honor the Son of the "Father of lights." At the beginning of his gospel, John tells about the event: "In Him was life; and the life was the light of men." "All things were made by Him," he tells us—all creation—"and the light shineth in darkness; and the darkness comprehended it not." The next time you see Christmas lights, think of the wonder of the Light which all the world's darkness has not been able to dim.

Christmas lights are a wonderful symbol, found inside and outside most homes. They brighten trees and shrubbery in the yards, and they outline windows and doors.

Floodlights often play on lawn figures ranging in variety from celestial choirs to mufflered snowmen. Some displays are garish and overdone, possibly created with the idea of winning a contest or outdoing the neighbors. But in many cases the outdoor lighting is reverent and beautiful and appreciated by all who view it.

Lighted community trees also are a source of pleasure to many and all of us take interest and some pride in our national Christmas tree lighted each year in Washington, D. C., a custom started in 1924 and continued by succeeding Presidents. There is also the celebration of the lighting of the mammoth tree in Rockefeller Center, New York City, with hundreds of lights hanging from its branches.

Light is a natural symbol for the One whose birth brought such great changes to the world. The Psalmist poetically addresses God, "Thou coverest Thyself with light as with a garment."

Lights and candles have been used for centuries at Christmas to express joy in the celebration and to signify the coming of the Light. The candle-lit tree is a beautiful shining memory from the childhood of many older persons (but it *did* present a fire hazard).

Placing candles in the window to light the Christ Child on His way is a custom brought to this country from Germany, though the Irish also claim to have originated it. If a passing stranger is weary or in need, the candle is there to assure him a welcome. Lighted candles

43

in windows also beckon passing carollers to stop and sing in some communities. Those engaged in the ancient craft of candlemaking feared that their means of livelihood was coming to an end when electricity came into common use in Europe, but there is untold beauty in the glow of the candlelight, which man still appreciates, and the new interest in ornamental candles has kept a number of very old firms in business and thriving, particularly in France. Christmas candles account for most of their output. Decorated tapers, stubby candles in bright colors, large ones with the Nativity scene or madonna and child carved into the base, graceful cathedral and "stained glass" candles—all these are made, and there is even one in the shape of a manger with the glow inside representing the Christ Child.

The custom of having an oversized candle which glows for many hours probably comes from medieval Europe. A giant candle is placed on a protective base on the floor; it burns generously throughout the season, lighting all the festivities and observances through Twelfth Night.

Holiday candles of various sizes can be made in your own home, and many families enjoy this do-it-yourself activity. You begin by melting paraffin, then adding stearic acid or beeswax, next pouring the mixture into molds made from fruit-juice cans or milk cartons, and finally adding cord for wicks. If you prefer, you can add decorations to purchased candles. "Snow" candles are

made by whipping partially cooled wax with an egg beater, and applying the mixture to a base candle with a fork.

Our use of candles at Christmas may have come from the Jewish Hannukah festival, a happy December holiday commemorating the rededication of the Temple. Hannukah involves the lighting of eight candles, one each night, and is known as the Festival of Lights.

"The entrance of Thy words giveth light," the Psalmist said; "it giveth understanding unto the simple." Light has always been associated with learning and understanding. While Christmas is a time of tradition and looking back, it is also a time for us to look ahead, to stretch our minds, to gain new insights, to grow in understanding, in the knowledge of truth and of our fellow men.

And if we have received this light of illumination, responsibility is implied. "Ye are the light of the world. A city that is set on an hill cannot be hid. Neither do men light a candle, and put it under a bushel, but on a candlestick; and it giveth light unto all that are in the house. Let your light so shine before men, that they may see your good works, and glorify your Father which is in heaven" (*Matthew 5:15, 16*).

Almost every custom we have, every motif or symbol we use at Christmas, is an attempt to give expression to and demonstrate the truth that "God so loved the world that He gave His only begotten Son . . . ," the Light of the World. This, of course, is the reason for our celebrations.

God showed us the way to love and good will. He put light on our pathway, so that it would shine in our hearts, giving us a desire to show love and good will toward our fellow men, extending Christmas into all the year.

"In the beginning was the Word, and the Word was with God, and the Word was God. The same was in the beginning with God. All things were made by him; and without him was not any thing made that was made. In him was life; and the life was the light of men. . . . That was the true Light, which lighteth every man that cometh into the world."

—JOHN 1: 1-4, 8-9

THE GIFT OF THE BABY

JOY

THERE IS NO MORE JOYOUS SEASON OR FESTIVAL IN OUR calendar than Christmas. The gift of the Christ Child is joy, for no other person has brought such deep and lasting happiness to the hearts of men. The birth of any baby is almost always a signal for rejoicing, and especially so at Christmas, when "love came down" to earth!

49

No wonder the heavens could not keep silent when Jesus was born!

One of the strangely beautiful attitudes we adopt in our celebration of Christmas is that we remember the birth of Christ, still thinking of Jesus as a baby. In this way, Jesus' birth date is different from any other. When we honor mortal men and celebrate their birthdays, we do not picture them as infants but as adults, mature and facing responsibility.

When on December 25 we celebrate the birth of Christ, however, we honor an infant. The birthday of Jesus is different, and *He* has made the difference! The wonder of it all is that God chose to send His Son to earth in the same way every man appears: as a baby needful of love and care, and dependent upon others, to reveal His love, and to command our love, "for God so loved the world. . . ."

Because God chose this unusual way to reveal Himself to man, the birth of Jesus has hallowed all childhood, has taught us, too, the wisdom of "becoming as little children." And so Christmas is the day for nurturing in us childlike faith and love.

As people grow older, they sometimes decide to dispose of their decorations. Or they say that they will not "make any fuss about the holiday because Christmas is for children." There is no doubt about it—Christmas *is* a child-centered holiday. But those adults who enjoy it most do adopt the same spirit of excitement and enchantment that make this day such a great day for children. Who enjoys the dolls, the trains, the new puppies, the building toys more than the grown-ups? At this season it is quite all right for adults to engage in gaiety, to let "visions of sugarplums dance in their heads."

But Christmas is more fun when shared with little folks. Everyone enjoys a baby in the house at this time of year, and parents grow sentimental about "his first Christmas" even if baby only crumples the colored wrappings or blinks his eyes at the bright lights.

> *"Hang up the baby's stocking,*
> *Be sure you don't forget,*
> *For the dear little dimpled darling*
> *Hasn't seen Christmas yet!"*

Making Christmas truly meaningful as a spiritual holiday to small children is a challenge to parents. Youngsters enjoy the lights and the presents but perhaps cannot understand the theology involved in the occasion. They can grasp the idea of its being Jesus' birthday, but they may wonder why He receives no gifts.

Some families have found it wise to carry over family birthday traditions to the celebration of Jesus' birthday. Sometimes it is customary for the birthday child to find a ribbon or a balloon tied to his chair when he comes to breakfast on the morning of his birthday. So, on Christmas morning, an empty chair is decorated in the same way, and the explanation is given to the tiny children

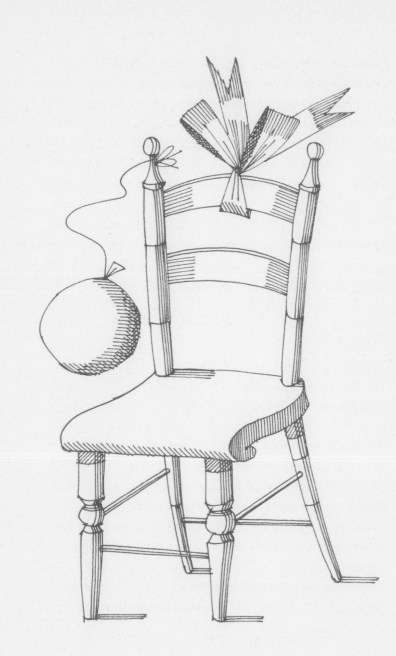

that this is Jesus' birthday. The youngsters sing "Happy birthday, dear Jesus," just as they would sing the song to a brother or sister. Or perhaps a special birthday cake for Jesus makes the day memorable. A large white-frosted cake is placed on the table with a single white or red candle in the center. The large candle represents the Lord Jesus. Sometimes there are small candles around the edge of the cake, one for each member of the family. With help, the children then light their own candles from the large center taper. There are several variations of this idea, each bringing new significance to the day for young minds and hearts.

One mother in Florida created a special Christmas cake to present the idea of Christ's birthday to her 6-year-old son. She prepared a cake with white frosting, placing on it a star made with silver dragees, a plastic angel, and twenty small red candles representing the centuries since the birth of Jesus.

The important thing in any festivity is to keep some phase of the observance simple enough so that even the youngest member of the family can participate meaningfully. As children grow older, they will find more and more to do in the preparations and celebrations. You need not look far to find pleasant projects. Youngsters love to "help" in the kitchen and Christmas can have greater significance for them if do assist with the seasonal baking. And as they do this, you can point out that many of our traditional Christmas foods, prepared from year to year by our mothers and their mothers before them, have a religious significance.

For instance, fruit cakes and plum puddings with their rich ingredients were at one time considered symbolic of the gifts of the Wise Men. A child helping to cut up citron, dates and nuts for the fruitcake will be interested in hearing again how the sages of the East

saw the star and followed it across the desert until they found the Child. He can be told that these Kings from the Orient probably carried fruits with them to eat on their long journey. Nuts and fruits were often presented as gifts in Biblical days, so it is quite possible that the Wise Men brought these tokens along with the treasures that are recorded in the Bible story.

After cutting the fruit and nuts, the child may continue his part in the holiday baking by sifting flour mixed with spices. Meanwhile a game can be played— identifying cinnamon, ginger and nutmeg by their fragrance. Cinnamon is often mentioned in the Bible. Its source—the island of Ceylon, off the southern tip of India—was carefully kept secret for centuries.

While the origin of many holiday treats is lost, the shape of the swaddling clothes is remembered in the twisted German bread, *Christollen* (usually called *stollen*), and the Hungarian sweet bread, *vanyoka*, so called because of the braided stands of fruited dough. Seen less often, the German *Springerlie* cookies, with pictures, were at one time marked only with doves, lambs and angels, and *lebkuchen*, the spicy "life cakes," speak of the new life in Christ. But of all the shapes for Christmas cookies, the favorite is the star. The first star cookies were made in the Near East, where a star is the sign of a rising king.

Letting children help with the preparation of these and other holiday foods can add a great deal to the family spirit. Cookies can be cut in shapes that have special meaning to children. One little girl makes her cookies heart-shaped, because "she wants to give love at Christmas."

When the children are of different ages, each should be enabled to participate in holiday activities according to his own level of ability. As the children grow older, they can share more and more in the planning as well.

Every family has its own special holiday traditions, individual and personal things they do each year. One of the nicest of family traditions I know is a private Christmas Eve service, a service which is the most worshipful occasion of the year for them as a family. The father or an older child reads the Luke passage from the Bible, the children light candles, all sing familiar carols, and there is prayer. This family service is a brief and joyful one, full of reverence, a chief treasure to be stored away in the memory of a happy childhood.

Some families prefer a more formal service, with a litany prepared by the older children, others an informal storytelling or question time. Most prefer a worship center of some sort, gathering around a crèche, a candle display, a beautiful Christmas plant, or a lighted tree.

Another family reenacts the Nativity story, with both parents and children taking part. This family custom was started when their first child was in the cradle. For several years, with babies in the family, there was always a child small enough to be placed in the manger; later a doll was substituted. The father took the part of the donkey, carrying the child who played the role of Mary until the rider grew too big. Animals for the stable were toy lambs or family pets, sometimes a cat, a hamster, or even a pair of white mice. Children's imaginations are a wonderful attribute. Though today the two older children are grown-up teenagers, they still look forward to taking part in the family Christmas Eve service, and have now taken over a good deal of the preparation and the responsibility of performance. The program goes something like this:

Singing of Christmas carols (any except "Silent Night");

Lighting of Christmas candle and song, "Christmas Means Thinking of Jesus" (when they were smaller it was "Happy Birthday, Dear Jesus");

Reading of the Christmas story from Luke;

Reading of the Christmas story from Matthew;

Dramatization with Mary, Joseph, Baby and shepherds plus animals (sometimes one person plays two parts);

Prayers, each child and parent taking part;

Closing carol, "Silent Night."

This outline can perhaps be used as a basis for your own Christmas Eve service.

Parents may sometimes be concerned about the "gimme" attitude which Christmas seems to foster in children. This season provides many opportunities to teach them the joy of giving. Children may select a favorite toy or item of food to give to a less privileged child. They can give of their love and labor in home-made gifts for relatives and friends.

If a child feels he has nothing to give, he can be taught Christina Rossetti's lovely poem, which epitomizes the significance of the season:

"What can I give Him, small as I am?
If I were a shepherd I would give a lamb.
If I were a Wise Man I would do my part.
What I can I give Him—give Him my heart."

Adults, too, can give their hearts. Often gifts are made to poor children at this time of year in honor of the Christ Child. Time and gifts and talents may be given to foundling homes and children's hospitals, in the form of special parties and visits to help make children happy. There is great pleasure in seeing any children with their gifts, enjoying entertainment. But giving a gift to a child far away who is in real need is worthy of very serious consideration.

Christmas is an ideal time to take on the support of a needy child through one of the fine "foster parent" plans, in which a sponsor pays from $10 to $15 a month toward the support of a particular child abroad. You then have the privilege of corresponding with the child. This is a fine gift to give children—an "adopted" brother or sister in an orphanage overseas or a poverty-touched home in a distant land.

It is also a splendid thing to make a special gift at

Christmas to a charity which helps children—a fresh air camp, a crippled children's hospital, a home for the mentally retarded or a milk fund. Much pleasure is to be had from the giving.

There are other gifts which may appropriately be given in honor of the Christ Child. A contribution to an organization helping Jewish people is a fine way for Christians to remember the birth of their Saviour who came from the line of David. Another might be a gift to needy mothers. In the mountains of Formosa primitive maternity hospitals have been set up, with trained nurses assisting the tribeswomen at the time of birth, and giving instruction in hygienic baby care. Americans give regularly to support these "rooms for Mary" in honor of Jesus' mother. Each mother is given a layette, and often it is the only clothing she has for her child. This type of giving heightens our own appreciation of the Day of the Baby.

To enter fully into the spirit of Christmas, as to enter the Kingdom of Heaven, we need to "become as little children." What delight we can find in simple pleasures of the season, what a glow we can carry about because of the warmth and kindness of friends and strangers, if we approach the holiday with the attitude of a child.

If God had appeared to mankind in human form as a full-grown man we could never feel quite as close to Jesus as we do. But He is an all-wise God and chose to reveal Himself in the form of a baby, whose gift to us is the gift of joy.

> *"I bring you good tidings of great joy,*
> *which shall be to all people.*
> *For unto you is born this day in the*
> *city of David a Saviour, which*
> *is Christ the Lord."*
>
> —LUKE 2: 10, 11

> *"Joy to the world*
> *The Lord is come*
> *Let earth receive her King!"*
>
> —ISAAC WATTS HYMN BASED ON PSALM 98; TUNE "ANTIOCH" BY GEORGE FREDERICK HANDEL, AN ARRANGEMENT FROM "THE MESSIAH."

MUSIC

WE ARE NOT TOLD SPECIFICALLY THAT THE ANGELS "sang," but the message they delivered to the shepherds is so lyrical that it must have been accompanied by heavenly music: "Glory to God in the highest, and on earth peace, good will toward men." The melody of the words has echoed and re-echoed through the years, with people of all lands singing "Gloria in excelsis deo" in every tongue of mankind. The gift of the angels was the glorious gift of music.

The shepherds on the hillside that night were startled when the angel appeared unto them with the message, "Unto you is born . . . a Saviour." And when the angel was joined by "a multitude of the heavenly host, praising God," they must have rubbed their eyes and wondered if they were seeing a vision.

No, they were not, for they saw the heavenly host with their own eyes, and they heard the sound of voices with their own ears—wonderful, vibrant words, "Glory to God in the highest. . . ." Like music to their ears was this prophecy come true.

This glorious and triumphant heavenly concert was presented to a group of humble shepherds on a hillside, not to an élite audience within the town nearby. They were working men who were doing nothing more spectacular than their duty, tending their flocks by night. Perhaps they were the only ones awake at that time, but even so they did expect this phenomenon. The nature of their tasks required watchfulness, and so they were alert when the angel and the heavenly host appeared, and they alone heard the angel chorus missed by everyone else in the town of Bethlehem.

That holy night and what it brought to mankind has been the subject of song throughout the ages. The minor music of pre-Christian days gave way at last to joyous major chords, and music and the "glad tidings of great joy" have affected all of life ever since.

Today around the world the singing of carols is one of the happiest aspects of the Christmas season, and is engaged in by people in all occupations. Groups of nurses go through the corridors of hospitals singing Christmas cheer to their patients; children tramp through snow to sing outside the windows of elderly shut-ins; church choirs spend hours rehearsing carols for candlelight carol services. Voluntary choruses and semi-professional groups carol in railroad stations, business offices and stores. At Christmastime, music, beautiful music fills the air.

On dignified streets of towns and cities little groups of carollers pass each other on their way to sing at candle-lit windows, the signal that carolling will be appreciated. Tiny hamlets in remote places hold carol-sings around their community trees. Christmas goes singing across our land, and around the world.

The first composer of Christmas songs (the term "carol" was not used until later) is believed to have been Aurelius Prudentus, a Spaniard of the fourth century who composed tunes and words for Latin hymns. The word itself comes from the French *carole,* a circle dance dating from the twelfth century.

By the 1300's, carols were sung in England for

worship, pageants, feasting and hunting. Some of the songs were inspired by the Nativity and Epiphany plays presented by travelling troupes.

Ballads developed in the following two centuries, by which time the term "carol" was applied specifically to Christmas songs, both secular and sacred. Church music had long been the exclusive privilege of the clergy. But carols were spontaneous expressions of joy, arising from the people's need to express their deep delight and awe in the coming of the Saviour. Though some carols were written by clergymen, they were really songs of the people.

The earliest printed collection of carols was made by Wynkyn de Worde in 1521. His book included the secular English carol known as "Boar's Head Carol." Probably the first carols to appear in England were lullabies, natural enough for a holiday honoring a Baby. Lullaby carols are popular in many countries; among them are "Jesu Bambino," "Away in a Manger," "Lullay Thou Little Tiny Child," and "Silent Night."

Most of the carols we sing today are English or European in origin, and Americans take delight in the universality of the Christmas spirit by joining our hearts with countries through the use of their songs. Several of our carols are entirely American, including Negro and white spirituals.

The first Christmas carol written on the American continent was probably an Indian song in the language of the Hurons of lower Canada. In 1641 Father Jean de Brébeuf, a French missionary to the Indians, wrote a six-stanza Christmas song titled *"Jesous Ahatonhia"* ("Jesus is born"), and set it to a sixteenth-century French melody that sounded a little like "God Rest You Merry, Gentlemen." When the Iroquois overran the Huron territory, the priest and many of his converts were captured and burned at the stake. But the hymn was preserved by Hurons who escaped into Quebec and Michigan, and it was later written down by missionaries. It has never become generally known in English.

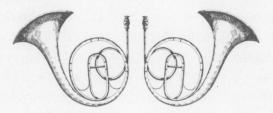

For years most people considered the beloved carol of childhood, "Away in a Manger," to be an old German carol written by Martin Luther. Many songbooks list it as "Luther's Cradle Hymn." However, the lullaby is unknown in Germany except where it has been taken by American or British travellers. "Away in a Manger" may have originated with the German Lutherans in Pennsylvania and was perhaps later taken to England, where it is popular today. The earliest record of the hymn is in a book titled *Little Children's Book: for Schools and Families,* published in 1855 by the Evangelical Lutheran Church of North America. Only the first two stanzas appear, and no author's name is given. On a facing page is a painting by Gustave F. L. Koenig showing Luther and his family at Christmas, and it was this association of word and picture that apparently gave rise to the theory that Luther had written the song for his children.

Two years later, in 1857, a book called *Dainty Songs for Little Lads and Lasses* was printed, and it contained the song, titling it "Luther's Cradle Hymn," adding that it was "composed by Martin Luther for his children and still sung by German mothers to their little ones." The compiler of the book must have used his imagination to arrive at this conclusion, though it may be true that the poem had been part of a play or story for children dealing with the life of Luther. While its first appearance in print was in English, the carol was promptly translated into German for use in Lutheran services, many of which used the German language at that time.

We are indebted to J. R. Murray's *Dainty Songs,* however, for our most popular tune for "Away in a Manger." In 1921 this tune was ascribed to Carl Mueller, Luther's brother-in-law, but there is no verification of this. The carol acquired a third stanza by another anonymous author between the years 1855 and 1892. Another melody to which this carol is often sung is that of "Flow Gently, Sweet Afton," by James E. Spillman.

Luther did write a Christmas carol for his sons— *"Von Himmel Hoch"* ("From Heaven Above I Come to You") around 1535. The tune was later arranged by Bach and the hymn was greatly beloved in Germany and among German descendants in America.

An American carol is the popular "It Came Upon a Midnight Clear," written on a snowy December day in 1849 by a Unitarian minister in Wayland, Massachusetts, Dr. Edmund Hamilton Sears. The poem was printed in a magazine titled *Christian Register,* published in Boston, and in 1850 set to the now-familiar tune composed by Richard Store Willis, a Bostonian.

This carol has a message for those who are "bent beneath life's crushing load," and offers rest to those whose steps are slow and painful "on the weary road." It is interesting to note that some people were almost as concerned about the need for world peace at mid-nineteenth century as we are today.

And in spite of its rather philosophical theme, this carol has always appealed to children. I can remember singing "the earth in Solomon stillness lay" before I could read or understand the word "solemn."

"We Three Kings of Orient Are," one of the few hymns specially arranged for dramatic presentation, was written in 1857 by the Reverend John Henry Hopkins,

Jr., rector of Christ Church, Williamsport, Pennsylvania, an Episcopal clergyman who wrote both the words and music. Few Christmas pageants are complete without this song and its dramatic possibilities. Now it appears in many church hymnals and is a beloved Sunday School song. Children love the air of mystery evoked by the minor melody of the verses and the switch to major in the refrain.

At least one Christmas carol was written on Christmas Day. The words for "I Heard the Bells on Christmas Day" came from the pen of Henry Wadsworth Longfellow on December 25, 1863, only six months after the Battle of Gettysburg. Longfellow's son had been injured in battle, and it is easy to see why he felt that "hate is strong, and mocks the song of peace on earth, good will to men."

This poem, which Longfellow called "Christmas Bells," was not published until 1867, when the war was over, and it did not acquire its present melody until 1872. The music was composed by J. Baptiste Calkin, a great English organist, and the last four measures of this tune are taken from an old "Amen." In "I Heard the Bells," Longfellow offers his personal experience of despair and hope. From " 'There is no peace on earth,' I said," he goes on to "God is not dead, nor doth He sleep; the wrong shall fail, the right prevail." Sometimes we are a little embarrassed at the words "peace on earth, good will toward men" when our cold war threatens to explode into nuclear disaster, and when our extended hand of friendship is scorned or slapped aside. Yet the very idea that peace and good will is desired by so many of the world's people is in itself comforting. We can take courage therefore from this experience of one of America's most beloved poets of the past.

Phillips Brooks, popular young minister of Holy Trinity Episcopal Church in Philadelphia, was greatly moved when he visited the Holy Land in 1865. On his return he attempted to share his impressions with his parishioners. One of his most vivid memories was of Christmas Eve spent in Bethlehem. Dr. Brooks later wrote a Christmas poem for the children of his church about the village where Jesus was born, which had been so much in his thoughts ever since his trip. The church organist, Lewis Redner, composed a tune for the poem in his sleep—at least it is said that the entire tune came into his head while he slept, and that he arose to write it down. The following Sunday the youngsters in Holy Trinity Sunday School were taught a new Christmas song, "O Little Town of Bethlehem." Their carol first appeared in a hymnal in 1892 and has been joyfully sung ever since, translated into many languages.

The little Arab town so near the barbed wire which today separates the Hashemite Kingdom of Jordan from the State of Israel still represents hopes and fears of many years. It looks peaceful at night from the surrounding hills, but the sentries who guard the border and the complications of crossing are reminders that the Prince of Peace does not rule there.

Even for those of us who have not seen it in person, the Holy Land—and Bethlehem in particular—seems a little closer when we sing Phillips Brooks' thoughtful carol. The young minister was so successful in transmitting the emotions of his visit that we still experience the joy and wonder of his Bethlehem visit.

Another American carol is Josiah G. Holland's "There's a Song in the Air," written in 1872. Dr. Holland was a remarkable man—a graduate of a medical college, a teacher, lecturer, writer and editor. His column, "Timothy Titcomb's Letters" in the Springfield (Massachusetts) *Republican,* was later published as a book, and he also wrote a novel and several volumes of poems. The versatile Dr. Holland is possibly best known as the founder and editor of *Scribner's Monthly.*

His Christmas poem was an immediate success when read to his Sunday School children, but it did not have a melody for many years afterward. In 1905 when a new Methodist hymnal was being published, three composers were invited to write tunes for the sprightly verse. Each was judged so good that all three were included in the hymnbook. The one most often sung today, however, was composed by Karl Harrington, a Latin professor at Wesleyan University at Middletown, Connecticut.

Several of our most moving carols cannot be traced

to an author, but come to us as traditional folk songs. "Go, Tell It On the Mountains" has a great deal of evangelical fervor and reflects the joy of the slave in the celebration of Christmas. It appeared in 1909 in *Religious Folk Songs of the Negro*, which was arranged from an original edition titled *Cabin and Plantation Songs as Sung by the Hampton Students*, published in 1874. No Negro spirituals were written down at all until the 1860's, and few were recorded before 1880. "Go Tell It On the Mountains" may possibly be of later origin than some, since the opening bars sound somewhat like "Tramp, Tramp, Tramp," and it may have been influenced by this George F. Root song so popular during the Civil War.

"Sweet Little Jesus Boy" is a poignant lullaby mirroring the sadness of the Negro's own position—"They didn't know who You was." "Rise Up, Shepherd an' Foller," a simple and direct spiritual, almost antiphonal, is reminiscent of the shepherd songs of the mystery plays.

Counting songs are an interesting form of carol. "Children, Go Where I Send You" (Little Bitty Baby) seems to be Southern Negro in origin, though popular also in the mountain areas among whites. The antiphonal form and additions to each stanza would be easy to use in a group of persons who could not read. The song goes rather far afield from the Christmas story—with Paul and Silas, those who "didn't get to Heaven"

73

and the Ten Commandments—but each stanza ends with the "little bitty Baby of Bethlehem."

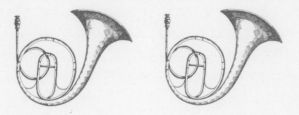

In the Southern mountains of the United States a number of old ballads carried from Scotland and Ireland by their ancestors are still sung by the older residents, many in quaint English. The "Cherry Tree Carol" in its Appalachian form has become quite popular through recordings and frequent performance by musical groups. The ballad itself is very old and has been traced to the European miracle plays. Based on an Apocryphal account in which Mary and Joseph fled to Egypt before Jesus' birth, the story has many versions with the fruit of the title adapted to the climate. The "cherry" is English, but the ballad has an "apple" in Spain, and has also appeared with the "date," "fig" and "coconut."

An old lullaby from the Southern highlands of the United States which retains old English words, "Lullay, Thou Little Tiny Child," known as the "Coventry Carol" (sometimes "Carol of the Mothers of the Innocents") was probably sung in a fifteenth-century English mystery play, the Pageant of the Shearman and Tailors. Court records tell us that Margaret of Anjou, Henry VI's queen, attended the Coventry Mystery plays in 1456. A text of the song made over by a Robert Croo is dated 1534, so the original was probably much older.

We can hardly call these American songs, but our highlanders are responsible for having preserved them. In Europe they have died out long ago, yet here they are still being sung in the stilted Elizabethan English in use when the settlers first came to this country. Isolated as they were from progress and changing American culture, they passed these songs on from one generation to another verbally. It is fortunate that these lovely carols now have been recorded in written form because the old people who sang them are passing on. The songs have a universality that makes them appealing today as they will always be.

Though it is Anglo-Saxon in spirit, "I Wonder As I Wander" is American, coming from the Appalachians. It is a true "white spiritual"; the tone of the song is quiet and reverent, the grammar obsolete, but its charm and simplicity is compelling. The song is often associated with the great contralto Marian Anderson, but it is not a Negro song.

The most popular of all carols, "Silent Night," comes to us from Austria. The oft-told story of Franz Gruber and Joseph Mohr and the broken church organ is a familiar one. The simple song composed for women's voices with guitar accompaniment was introduced to this country by a troupe of Tyrolean singers on concert tour. Since 1811 the carol has appeared in American hymnals, apparently losing very little in translation. And we still enjoy hearing the German version, "Stille Nacht, Heilige Nacht," long associated with the beloved Schumann-Heink.

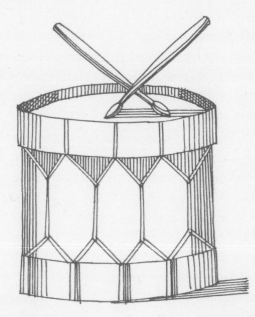

The voice is not the only means of giving expression to the joy of Christmas. Many musical instruments also have a special part in Christmas celebrations—drums, for example, along with trumpets and other horns, ancient lutes and mandolins. "Carol of the Drums" is an old Czech folk carol with its modern counterpart, "The Little Drummer Boy."

Moravian holiday worship has always included horns, especially trombones. In Bethlehem, Pennsylvania, the trombone choir climbs to the tower of Old Moravian Church on Christmas morning to play "How Brightly Shines the Morning Star," then continues the music while marching through the principal streets.

Harps are also suited to Christmas—and not just because of their association with angels! They are often used in special carol services. Organ recitals, too, and recordings of Christmas organ music are popular. Churches using loud-speaker systems can add to "the song in the air" by broadcasting organ and carillon music at Christmas in their communities. Bells, too, have their role in the season's festivities. There is just something Christmassy about the sound of bells, and thus they are inseparably related to the holiday. This is one Christmas symbol which has never been disapproved as heathenish.

In medieval England church bells rang out each Sunday during the Advent season. Later, on the three mornings preceding Christmas and on Christmas Eve at sunset, the melody of the great bells filled the air.

Another tradition was the Devil's Knell or Old Lad's (Devil) Passing, a somber tolling of bells just before midnight Christmas Eve, giving way at the stroke of

midnight to joyful ringing. Church bells have always been more important in England and on the Continent than in the United States. England has been called "the ringing island" because of them, and Australia and New Zealand have carried on this tradition of their mother country. One of the best-loved Christmas hymns was inspired by such ringing of the bells on Christmas morning, Charles Wesley's carol, "Hark the Herald Angels Sing" originally written "Hark, how all the welkin rings."

Contemporary churches in the United States seldom have traditional church bells, although many are equipped with electronic carillons. There is a type of bell ringing, however, which today is becoming increasingly popular among talented young people in church groups: it is handbell ringing. When the lighting of the trees on New York City's Park Avenue takes place in early December each year, it is a community event with the street closed to traffic while people of diverse backgrounds stand together to sing the beautiful Christmas carols—and they are accompanied by the handbell-ringers from the Brick Presbyterian Church. Handbell ringing requires skill and precision, especially when the ringers handle two or three bells simultaneously. Bells, a wonderful Christmas symbol, are seen everywhere at this season, hanging across streets, on front doors, as tree ornaments, on greeting cards. They are a symbol of joy and of witnessing, bringing a message of good will,

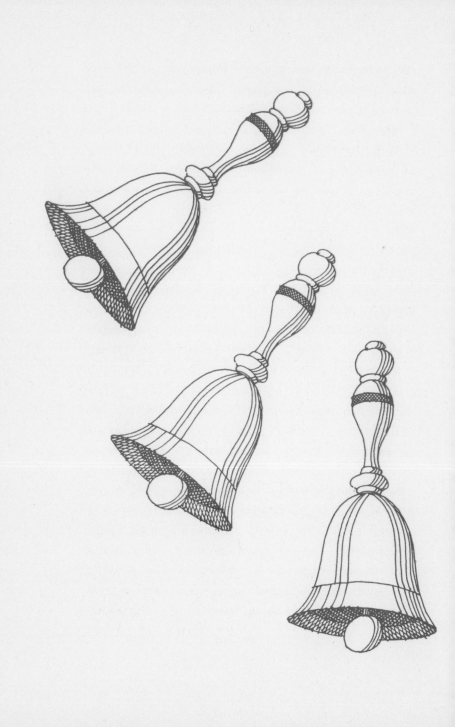

calling the people to worship, echoing the triumphant song of the angels, "Glory! Glory to God in the highest!"

The theme of the coming of Christ has inspired some of our most beautiful classical music. What would Christmas be without Handel's *Messiah!* Usually only the "Christmas" portion is sung at this season, but the Hallelujah Chorus has become as much a part of the holiday as Adeste Fidelis. In the more than 200 years since its first performance in Dublin, *The Messiah* has sung its way around the world and today is possibly the most universal of Christmas compositions. Indeed, the highlight of a travel film seen by millions of persons several years ago was the Hallelujah Chorus sung by a choir of Tonga Islanders.

Johann Sebastian Bach's lyrical *Christmas Oratorio* is another greatly loved composition which has stood the test of time. Saint-Saens' *Christmas Oratorio* and Berlioz' *L'Enfance du Christ* are regularly performed at this season to the delight of thousands.

But not all Christmas classics are centuries old. Along with Bach's *Magnificat* we revere Vaughn Williams' *Fantasia on Christmas Carols*. Some of the new music only appears to be ancient. The contemporary British composer, Benjamin Britten, in his *A Ceremony of Carols,* welds quaint old English verses to tunes which sound medieval, yet modern. Each year more choirs perform this remarkable composition, happily singing the strange-sounding words. Many contemporary cantatas combine the old and new, as do Honegger's *Christmas Cantata* and Holtz' *Christmas Day* with their interweaving of old carols.

A good example of a modern classic is Gian Carlo Menotti's *Amahl and the Night Visitors*. First performed in 1951, this was the first opera created specifically for television. By now perhaps more children know this version of the story of the Wise Men than the Biblical one. It has become, in a few years, a significant part of our American Christmas culture. In music, as in other phases of our Christmas celebration, we cling to the traditional, yet make room for the new when it has meaning for us.

Can you imagine a Christmas without music? Scarcely! Christmas is a time to sing for joy, and whether or not we can carry a tune, we can keep our *hearts* in tune. We can "make melody in our hearts unto the Lord." We can give glory to God in the Highest.

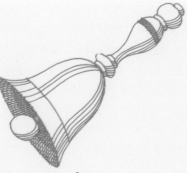

*"We hear the Christmas angels the great glad
        tidings tell;
O come to us, abide with us Our Lord Emmanuel."*

—O LITTLE TOWN OF BETHLEHEM

*"And suddenly there was with the angel a multitude of
the heavenly host praising God, and saying, Glory to
God in the highest, and on earth peace, good will toward
men."*

—LUKE 2:13, 14.

REMEMBRANCE

CHRISTMAS IS A TIME OF REMEMBERING, OF REMEMBER-
ing what happened in Bethlehem that very first Christmas, of remembering childhood and family celebrations.
Our own observance of this beautiful holiday is made
up of these personal memories plus the accretions of the
years.

From time to time we hear—and perhaps we sometimes voice—complaints about the secularization of Christmas or the pagan origins of its traditions. Comfortingly, the attempts of many individuals and groups to emphasize the religious aspects have borne fruit; as a people we are becoming increasingly aware of Christmas as the birth of Christ. We are remembering its true significance.

It is certain that many of our present-day practices and customs had their origin in the worship of Odin, the Druids or the gods of Rome. Over the centuries, however, many of these traditions have acquired new significance for new eras, carrying with them new meaning for many of us.

The use of mistletoe is one example. It was a sacred plant in northern Europe, considered so powerful that if enemies met under the vine's overhanging branches they would not fight but would instead separate peaceably. Through the ages it has had special significance for the young; many a girl has hopefully hung the mistletoe to give her shy swain courage to kiss her. In some areas this plant was forbidden in the church because of its heathen connections, but in others it was a part of the holiday decoration with a sanctified significance. The priest started the holy kiss of peace and pardon under the mistletoe, which was passed on through the congregation to heal many a rift and contention—a superstitious thing turned to good.

One may also hear complaints about the designation of December 25 as Christmas, because this coincides with the Roman Saturnalia, a feast celebrated with debauched revelry. Today most scholars agree that it is unlikely that the birth of Jesus occurred in winter. It is improbable, though not impossible, that sheep would be kept on the Judean hills on a December night; they are usually inside the stables at that time of year. Our lovely songs about the snow and the bleak midwinter have more to do with northern Europe than with Jordan.

In the first two centuries after Christ's coming His followers were looking eagerly for His promised second advent and gave no thought to celebrating the date of His birth. Besides, this was not a common practice at the time. The death dates of great men were celebrated, not their birth dates.

By 245, however, the impetus for a celebration of the Nativity had started. The philosopher-theologist, Origen, objected to this, insisting that it was a sin to think of keeping the birthday of Christ "as though He were a king Pharaoh." But the idea spread in spite of Origen's objections, though a date could not be agreed upon. In some areas it was celebrated as late as April. Armenia, the first country to declare itself a Christian nation, settled on January 6 as the date, and they still keep it as the birthday of Jesus (though the difference in calendars makes this our January 7).

By the middle of the fourth century, Christians in

Rome were keeping December 25. Chrysostom wrote, in the 380's, "On this day also the birthday of Christ was lately fixed at Rome in order that while the heathen were busy with their profane ceremonies the Christians might perform their sacred rites undisturbed."

The Saturnalia was concerned with the winter solstice and the departure of the sun, recognized by the Romans as essential to life. At this period the sun appears to turn toward the earth again, so this was reason for rejoicing. Christians felt this a good time to witness to their neighbors that the real source of life, the Sun of Righteousness, is Jesus Christ, and so they celebrated Saturnalia in their own way.

When Christianity became the state religion an attempt was made to make December 25 a completely religious holiday, but it was a long time before the pagan elements of the celebrations died out. As late as 743 St. Boniface, known as "the apostle to the Germans," complained to Pope Zacharias about the sordid carnivals celebrated by the Christians in Rome.

Theological considerations also led to the selection of December as the time of Christ's birth. Theologians of the early centuries decided that Jesus must have lived an even (or "perfect") number of years from conception to death. The time of His death was certain—in the Spring at the Passover season. So figuring back, they reasoned that the conception occurred about the same time of year, making the birth date late December.

Clement of Alexandria, a fifth-century church father, made reference to the celebration, but the name *Christmas,* deriving from the mass held at midnight on Christmas Eve, is no older than the twelfth century. The word is distinctly English. Most European countries call the holiday The Nativity or Christ's Birthday, though Scandinavians have held to the pagan title Yule Day. Of course they were the last Europeans to receive Christianity—in the tenth century, four hundred years after Augustine had gone to evangelize England.

Today most of those who celebrate Christmas keep it on December 25. The Russian and Syrian Orthodox churches prefer January 6, and the Abyssinian (Coptic) Church celebrates on January 23. In the Church of the Nativity at Bethlehem, Jordan, services are held on all three Christmases with a great deal of rivalry among the priests.

Which date we celebrate as Jesus' birthday seems to me to be immaterial; what is important is that we keep *some* date for remembrance of this greatest event in human history. But since we are unable to determine the actual date (accurate birth records are fairly recent even in our own country), it seems hardly worth a quarrel with others who are worshipping at the same manger.

Whatever our traditions, each of us—or each family —celebrates in his own way. It would be difficult to find two families who do exactly the same things at Christmas. And our traditions grow uniquely as we add observances meaningful to us.

Have you ever thought what it would be like to have no Christmas traditions? How would you go about keeping Christmas if you had never before celebrated the birth of Christ? This has happened to many new Christians in countries which do not have a Christian culture. Where missionaries and other Westerners have gone they have carried their own national and family traditions filtered through their personal judgment and prejudices. Adaptations of many kinds have been made to the local situation, yet Christmas is recognizable wherever Christians gather.

Pageants are presented by Sunday School children in Tanganyika and Iceland with the same delight as in America. The animals sharing the stable may not be sheep and cows, but the message is unchanged. Carols sung in Korean are, if anything, even more beautiful than when sung in English.

A parade through the streets to the church, banners flying, was a feature of early Christmases in China. Since it was a regular business day for everyone except the Christians, they took this way of witnessing to their neighbors before joining in a happy service and "family" meal together at the church.

Our own Navajos who live on reservations are relatively untouched by our commercial American Christmas. Sometimes a big dinner is held at the trading post, with clothes and toys, fruits and candies for all who attend. "Kismus" is a vital and vibrant day though many Indians have not grasped its significance.

Most of our Christmas customs come from England, Holland or Germany. Mention of Charles Dickens and "merrie olde England" brings to our minds a time of feasting, slightly rowdy drinking, hanging of the greens, mistletoe and holly, sharing with the poor, wassailers singing from door to door, general good fellowship. The first celebration of Christmas in England was said to have been in 521, when King Arthur celebrated his victory in taking York. Holidays were gay during the Norman period, but the observance was banned while Oliver Cromwell was in power because the jollity had led to excesses. Refraining from work on Christmas, unless it fell on Sunday, was a punishable offense.

The Puritans who came to our shores in 1620 carried these same convictions—or at least their leaders did. According to Governor Bradford's diary, the people were hard at work putting up the first house for common use on December 25. A year or so later several of the company objected to work on Christmas "on religious grounds," so were released to attend to their devotions. When the Governor found them playing and enjoying sports instead of praying, however, he sent them back to their tasks.

Gay Christmas customs arrived with other settlers and before many years had passed, public expression of happiness returned to the season. Today most Christians feel that there is a place for both solemnity and laughter.

Most of our Christmas carols are a heritage from England, as are many of our favorite stories. The all-time favorite, one which gravely influenced the celebrations of the period, is Dickens' "A Christmas Carol." For some, the top-hatted and mufflered carollers under the lamp post—depicted on so many greeting cards—signify Christmas as much as the Wise Men kneeling at the manger. And Tiny Tim's "God bless us every one" is as much a part of the holiday as "Merry Christmas!" This greeting itself is English. We don't wish anyone a merry anything else. Merry is seldom used in conversation, yet it is on everyone's lips at this season.

Christmas cards originated with the English, though German bakers did make large cookies with frosted greetings, and sent them to special customers. The first Christmas greeting card was probably made in the 1840's. By 1858 or 1859, cards were for sale, though quite expensive. The Marcus Card Company soon after introduced Christmas cards to the United States, where they were immediately popular. Louis Prang, a Boston lithographer, started a card business in 1874, and by 1881 was turning out five million cards a year of excellent quality and design, producing them in 20 colors.

Our great debt to Holland is for St. Nicholas, who has undergone quite a transformation by becoming Santa Claus. And in this latter form he has become a world figure in his own right, known throughout all the lands.

Hollanders celebrate St. Nicholas Day on December 6, as do most Europeans, and it is a very special day for children. The night before, the good saint—wearing red bishop's robes and accompanied by an assistant known as Black Peter—visits homes, leaving either gifts or switches for the children, depending on their behaviour. Children put out shoes filled with straw for the horse on which St. Nicholas rides; and in the morning they find, in return, candies and gifts. Spicy ginger cookies shaped and frosted to look like Black Peter delight the youngsters.

The mythical saint is derived from a very human one, whose grave you may see today when you visit Turkey.

Nicholas, Bishop of Myra, in Asia Minor, was a fourth-century church official known for his kindness and fair judgment. He came from a wealthy family, but early went into the service of the church. The story is told that when Nicholas learned of the plight of an impoverished nobleman unable to provide a dowry so that his eldest daughter could be married, he went to the man's house secretly and threw a bag of gold in the window. The nobleman was overjoyed at the unexpected good fortune and his daughter was promptly married to her suitor. When it was time for the second daughter to be married, again there was no money for a dowry. The same thing happened this time. When the youngest of his three daughters wanted to marry, the nobleman kept watch several nights in the garden and this time he saw Nicholas throwing in the bag of gold. Nicholas was unhappy to be discovered and swore the man to secrecy. Somehow the word got out and the bishop became a legend in his own lifetime.

(The three bags of gold also became a symbol. They turned up on the coat of arms of the powerful Medici family of Florence, and today we can still see them, rounded into balls, hanging outside the pawnshop. When we look at them we should be reminded of the generosity of this fourth-century bishop.)

The western church took kindly to the veneration of the bishop, and he holds a place in the hearts of many different peoples including mariners, which accounts for the ships in Christmas lore, as in "I saw three ships come sailing in." The story of St. Nicholas came to America with the good burghers who settled "Nieuw Amsterdam," and the new land was a good place for it to flourish. Like the varied peoples who came to these shores, shaped and changed by the land itself, so the solemn bishop with red robes and miter underwent a transition through the writings and drawings of a new nation.

Clement Moore, an Episcopalian minister and seminary professor living in Manhattan, is credited with the greatest influence in the making of Santa. In his poem "The Night Before Christmas" he described a jolly, red-cheeked little man dressed in a red suit trimmed with white fur. The cartoons of Nast changed the "jolly old elf" to a fullgrown man, filling out his dimensions to his present ample silhouette.

Santa Claus, a decidedly American institution, is one of our most popular exports. In New Zealand, where Christmas comes at the hottest time of the year, department store Santas perspire in red-and-white costumes while listening to childish requests. Even Tokyo has white-bearded Santa Clauses in its large stores. And Santa is such an important figure on the American scene that many feel the true meaning of Christmas is lost in his shadow. We need to see behind the ho-ho-ing figure to the wealthy young man of the Middle East who gave up a life of idleness to serve God and the church, and who was known all through his life for his gentleness and goodness.

Martin Luther was much concerned with the influence of St. Nicholas upon the people of his church. Not at all sympathetic with the worship of saints, he attempted to turn the people's attentions to the Christ Child. In Germany, gifts are brought to children on Christmas Eve by the Christ Child. Many charming Christmas customs have come from this land, where Christmas is whole-heartedly observed. Germany's greatest contribution to our holiday, however, is the gaily-decked Christmas tree.

There are various claims to the first Christmas tree in America, but quite unanimous agreement that the land of its origin was Germany. Some feel that the Hessian soldiers were celebrating with a tree when Washington and his men crossed the Delaware River and won so decisive a victory. It is a matter of record that a German professor at Harvard by the name of Charles Follen set up a tree in his home in 1832. Pastor Henry Schwan is believed to have set up the first church tree in Cleveland, Ohio, in 1851.

England first took up the custom when Prince Albert, Queen Victoria's German-born husband, set up a tree for the children in Windsor Castle in 1841. France also embraced the custom about this time. In our country, as late as the turn of the century, it was considered a custom of the German immigrants, not of the entire population. But today Christmas trees are to be found almost everywhere. Evergreens are grown on vast tree farms scientifically cultivated to provide for the vast demand.

The Christmas tree is to many a symbol of Christ, the tree of life, Who freely offers to all His gifts of light and life. Ansagarius, when preaching to the Vikings in the tenth century, is said to have described the balsam fir as "nearly as high as hope, as wide as love," and said that it bore "the sign of the cross on every bough." This evergreen is still a great favorite, although every imaginable variety has been used as a Christmas tree.

The custom of decorating trees goes back to the Paradise Plays of medieval days. December 24 was kept as Adam and Eve Day, and dramas were presented to commemorate the event. They were usually preceded by a parade through the streets with players carrying the tree. The plays featured the Tree of Life and the Tree of the Knowledge of Good and Evil, one trimmed with roses, the other with apples.

Still later, candles were added to the Tree of Knowledge to indicate enlightenment. In Hamburg, stores sold small figurines of Adam and Eve and the serpent. As time went on the tree became a part of the Nativity celebration and lost its former significance, turning only into a thing of beauty.

The first careful description of a Christmas tree appears in a travel book dated 1605: "At Christmas time in Strassburg they set up fir trees in the rooms, and they hang on them roses cut of many-colored paper, apples, wafers, gilt, sugar, and so on." In the 1740's a minister of Strassburg complained about the trees as a trifle "with which people occupy the Christmas time more than with God's Word . . . a bit of child's play."

By the middle of the nineteenth century the tree was a most important part of the German Christmas. Sometimes "Christ's tree" was hung in the window or from the rafters, decorated with paper, tin stars, cakes, apples and candles. Almost everything colorful has been used to trim Christmas trees. In Poland strings of mushrooms

are hung between paper flowers and birds made of egg shells. The tree in Serbia had to be topped with a bright apple with chicken feathers tucked into it. Scandinavians hang the tree with birds and angels made of straw, and early American trees were gay with strands of popcorn and cranberries.

In Italy the custom of hanging the tree with fruit has

continued. Fresh lemons, oranges, tangerines and huge grapes are placed on the tree and then are eaten on Christmas night. We call trees and wreaths decorated with fruit "Della Robbia style," because of the artist who created so many Nativity porcelains which included fruit and evergreens.

Several groups have condemned the use of Christmas

trees because of a passage in Isaiah telling of a tree decked with gold and silver which was worshipped by the pagan neighbors of the Israelites. But have you ever heard of a single person who *worshipped* a Christmas tree? Our American Christmas tree is a thing of great pleasure and artistic delight, not an object of worship. And it does have special significance for the Christian. The evergreen has long been a symbol of immortality. A live tree speaks of the continuing life that is in Christ which He passes on to His followers. When strung with lights it is a reminder of the Light of the World.

One of the brightest spots of color in our homes and churches at Christmas comes from the Poinsettia, for which we are indebted to our neighbor, Mexico. The United States Ambassador to Mexico in 1830, J. R. Poinsett, was impressed with the red flower the Mexicans called "flor de pascua," or Christmas flower. The blossom was small but interesting because it was somewhat star-shaped and the petals were red leaves surrounding a tiny yellow center. Ambassador Poinsett liked its brilliant color and sent back a plant to Bartram's Botanic Garden. The new plant interested horticulturists all over the country but it was a Philadelphia florist, Robert Buist, who first raised it commercially. It took years of improvement to produce the plant with the huge flowers we have today. San Diego County, the "Poinsettia capital of the world," grows over 90 per cent of all commercial Poinsettias. One 400-acre ranch along a main highway near the Pacific Ocean provides a breath-taking view for motorists when the brilliant flowers are in bloom.

All over the world where people keep Christmas they have customs that bring happiness and carry deep significance in the greater meaning of the day. Here in America we have the traditions of many lands and cultures. From the combination have come new traditions, now entirely our own. We, too, bring to the Christ Child the gift of remembrance.

Traditions and customs help us remember. Yet if necessary we could have Christmas with no decorations, no gaily trimmed trees, no sound of carols, no crèche, no festive board. Keeping Christmas is a matter of the heart.

During the early troubles with the Communists in China, two missionaries were captured while hurrying home from a preaching trip to spend Christmas with their families. They were placed in a small room with a guard, and all their possessions, including their Bibles, were taken away. Each hour, they realized, might be their last. They were forbidden to speak to each other, and a guard was there to enforce the rule.

As Christmas morning dawned, one of the men awakened. He was remembering past Christmases, visualizing the decorated chapel at his mission station and the early morning service, and he was concerned with the agony of worry his wife was feeling, uncertain whether this day would bring life or death. He looked across at his companion who had been ill during the night, and he desperately wanted to convey his Christmas greetings.

Suddenly he had an idea. The guard was idly looking out the window, so the missionary pulled pieces of straw from his mattress and with them spelled out a word for his friend to see—EMMANUEL.

The sick man's face lighted up. Emmanuel—*God with us!*—of course He was with them! What a difference this exchange made in the men's spirits that day!

The captors ultimately decided to release the men, and they returned to their joyful families and mission associates. But in all their Christmases afterward they remembered that day. They had learned the one essential for joy in the holiday—the remembrance of *why* we celebrate Christmas. Because God became man, that we might become like Him. And whether we have little or much of tradition and custom, this is the way to keep Christmas—by *remembering*.

Everywhere, everywhere, Christmas tonight!
Christmas in lands of the fir-tree and pine,
Christmas in lands of the palm-tree and vine,
Christmas where snow peaks stand solemn and white,
Christmas where corn fields stand sunny and bright.
Christmas where children are hopeful and gay,
Christmas where old men are patient and gray,
Christmas where peace, like a dove in his flight,
Broods o'er brave men in the thick of the fight;

Everywhere, everywhere, Christmas tonight!
For the Christ-Child who comes is the Master of all;
No palace too great, no cottage too small.

—PHILLIPS BROOKS

THE GIFT OF THE WISE MEN

THEIR BEST

TRADITION TELLS US THAT THE WISE MEN ARRIVED IN
Bethlehem on January 6, and this day has been celebrated for hundreds of years as Epiphany, the mani-
festation to the Gentiles. Epiphany also commemorates
the baptism of Jesus, an event remembered by the
Christian church long before the Nativity was honored.

In the early church there was a group which held that Jesus was born all-human, but became divine at His baptism. This is the reason that Epiphany was the most important day in the calendar after Easter. Another group of Christians insisted that Jesus was born both human and divine, which led to the celebration of the birth.

The Nativity celebration of the West eventually outshone the celebration of Epiphany of the Eastern Church, though the latter day was still greatly honored. In England, after the acceptance of Christianity, the entire twelve-day period was celebrated as a holiday, a time of feasting and gaiety. The custom apparently began with Alfred in the ninth century and continued through the Middle Ages.

In recent years there has been considerable revival of interest in the twelve days of Christmas, possibly brought about by the popularity of the old English carol of that title, now heard so often during the Christmas season. While few have any interest in receiving such gifts as "maids a-milking, lords a-leaping, swans a-swimming, French hens," or even the "partridge in a pear tree"—the song does remind us that there are twelve days between Christmas and Epiphany, and that they are a majestic part of Christmastide. In some communities there is a concerted attempt to celebrate the twelve days in a way that will enhance the spirit of Christmas for all.

In Cincinnati, the "Christ in Christmas Committee" makes suggestions each year for home and community activities, and these are well publicized through newspapers and posters. Through the years certain events have become traditional. The day after Christmas, teenagers are recognized; another day honors younger children. A day is given over to visitation of the lonely and handicapped, and yet another to hospitality. "Greet Christ in the Stranger" Day is a time for entertaining new neighbors, recent immigrants, international students and visitors. On December 31 they pray for peace. On one day a visit to the community Crib in a downtown park is suggested. On another day citizens are reminded of the Nativity display at the art museum, and of the colorful floral arrangements in the park conservatory. Visits to the public library's Christmas collection, and attendance at the library's story hours are recommended. Community sings are encouraged and suggestions are offered for home activities.

The season is climaxed on Twelfth Night with a procession and program. Representatives of other nations in their national costumes join the richly dressed Magi in paying homage to the Christ Child. After the march to the Crib, everyone proceeds to a nearby auditorium where highlights of Christmas celebrations and music of many lands are presented.

Wherever you may be, there are many happy ways for a family to extend the joys of Christmas into the days after December 25. Small children love a daytime party with neighborhood youngsters, and a birthday cake for Jesus can well be a feature of this.

Teen-agers enjoy and learn from a progressive dinner, with each course representing a different country. Simple decorations at each home symbolize Christmas in that country. The soup might be Hungarian, the salad Italian, pâté de nöel (glorified hamburger in a pie shell) for France, wassail (hot punch) for England, *lebkuchen* or other Christmas cookies for Germany. A carol from the particular country is sung at each stop and the hostess tells something of holiday-keeping in that land.

Boxing Day, December 26, is an old English occasion for presenting gifts to the poor and bonuses to those who have served well during the year. This is also known as St. Stephen's Day, immortalized in the carol "Good King Wenceslas." Children may enjoy acting the story of this carol about the good and devout Duke (not a real king) who ruled Bohemia from 928 to 935. They can also learn about Stephen, the first Christian martyr, whose story is told in the Book of Acts.

And what a delightful evening a group of musical adults or teenagers can have singing madrigals, an ancient music form with vocal parts all of equal value. Six or eight persons sit around a table singing without instrumental accompaniment. A number of Psalms and some carols have been arranged in madrigal form. If this is a very special party, possibly for members of the church choir, participants may want to wear improvised sixteenth- or seventeenth-century costumes.

If you have a wood-burning fireplace, this can be the focal point of the evening fun. The Yule log should be brought in with great ceremony—it may, of course, be any available log, tied with gay ribbons—and chemicals can be added to make the log glow different colors. The log is placed on the already-burning fire, and while it ignites someone explains that the Yule log is supposed to destroy all hatreds, envies and misunderstandings as it burns. Each member of the family should mentally throw into the fire all such ill feelings.

Families may want to set aside special days during this period just to have fun together. A family evening is especially appropriate for the seventh day of Christmas, January 1, which is celebrated in the church calendar as the day Jesus was given His name. We remember that Christ chose to be part of a family, and ever since He came families have had a special sort of glory. ". . . The Father, for whom every family in heaven and earth is named."

A wassail bowl is another important custom for this day. Prepare a hot fruit- or vegetable-juice punch. In the absence of a punch bowl, a large mixing bowl or cookie jar will do nicely. This can be carried around the rooms with all the children trooping after the one carrying it, all singing. The bowl can then be set in front of the fire to keep it warm. An old English custom, once the wassail bowl was set before the fire, was to hang apples on long strings from the top of the fireplace so that the juice dripped into the bowl as the apples roasted.

While sitting around the fireplace, light a tall candle, and start singing a familiar carol. Sing one line and pass the candle to the next person, who must sing the second line, and so on until the carol is finished. Be sure the songs are easy enough so that the youngest children may participate, and that their hands are protected from candle drippings.

Everybody in the family turns artist while they try

their hands (up to the elbow) at executing Christmas scenes in finger paint. Or if you are more artistically advanced, carve camels or angels or other Christmas figures from soap. (Mark the design before starting with the paring knife.) Mother can use the soap chips later, so that even failures are not a total loss. The most successful statuettes may warrant later coloring with oil paint.

Try the attic or Grandma's house and work up a fashion show of old-time clothes. Play old-fashioned parlor games. If grandparents are present, let them tell about their early Christmases while you pop corn, roast apples or toast marshmallows at the fire. A good way to wind up an evening of this sort is the reverent recital together of the prayer which begins, "Our Father . . ."

On New Year's Eve small children may feel cheated at not being allowed to stay up to welcome the New Year. Hold a special "watch night" service for them before their bedtime. Ask each member of the family to have a special New Year's resolution ready. Candles are set out on a table, one for each person, plus a large one already lighted. After a few words from a parent about God's blessing during the old year and the opportunities ahead in the new year, the youngest child picks up a candle, tells his resolution and lights his candle. The older children follow according to age, then mother and father. All sing a familiar hymn and someone prays for strength to keep the resolutions. If the children are not going to be wakened at midnight, serve hot choco-late and send them to bed with cries of "Happy New Year."

Twelfth Day or Epiphany is another good occasion for family festivity. Prepare an Epiphany Cake for dessert, frosted and wearing a crown of gum drops. This variation of the old English "Twelfth Cake" can be made with any favorite recipe. Before baking distribute through the batter: three hard beans (tokens of the three kings), a toothpick (minstrel's baton), a little star made of foil (for the astronomer) plus enough almonds to have a token for each person.

As the baked-in treasures are discovered the person in whose portion they appear takes on that character for the rest of the evening. Almonds represent slaves, who may choose such tasks as water carrying or camel driving if they like, but will really do the dishwashing and cleaning up. Allow about ten minutes for costuming from anything readily at hand.

Place three large chairs in a place of honor for the three kings. The minstrel leads the music; everyone sings Epiphany carols or he may sing a solo. Two carols appropriate for this day are William Dix's "As With Gladness Men of Old" and Reginald Heber's "Brightest and Best of the Sons of the Morning."

If the astronomer is a child who can read, he may either read aloud the story of the visit of the Magi from Matthew or retell it in his own words. If the star goes to a tiny child, let him hold it over the stable during the procession, later. There could be a discussion of the meaning of the Wise Men's search or older children might listen to the reading of a story, possibly a shortened version of Henry Van Dyke's *The Other Wise Man*. If you have records of "Amahl and the Night Visitors," this would be appropriate. Then with the three kings leading, all parade through the house singing "We Three Kings of Orient Are," ending their procession at the crèche. Here the kings present their "gifts," and all kneel while someone offers a prayer of dedication.

Gifts have long been associated with Twelfth Night. In Italy children receive gifts on Twelfth Night Eve, presents supposedly delivered by the Wise Men on their way through. Straw is put out for the camels in case they should be hungry, and it somehow always disappears by morning. In Syria children's gifts are supposedly delivered by a camel which was separated from the caravan and has been wandering around looking for the Magi.

Legends are charming and holiday make-believe is a part of our celebration, but we must never lose sight of the fact that there actually were men—we do not know how many—who came to see the Infant King. The fact that three gifts were mentioned—gold, frankincense and myrrh—has given rise to the idea that there were

three Wise Men. There may have been more, perhaps a whole party sent as a special mission from a small country of the East to pay homage to the new king of Judea. Or they may have had some mystical ideas of His kingdom. Whatever they thought, it probably was not as remarkable as the truth. We are told that this tiny baby was the King of Kings and Lord of Lords. Later He said, "My kingdom is not of this world . . .".

But what strange baby-gifts the Wise Men brought! Who would think of giving metal and spices to a baby? Of course these gift-bringers did not have the kind of stores we have in which to make their purchases. In those days gifts were usually of gold, clothing, jewelry or perfume spices. People had their "money" in possessions and valuables rather than currency.

The gold they brought may have been in the form of jewelry or beaten into a dish or plate. We can be sure it was a gift worthy of a king, however, for such is a gift of pure gold. Gold is a basis for economic standards. Our government, for instance, is worried when our country's gold supply decreases. As individuals, too, gold represents to us wealth, position and power—which few of us have. How could *we* present such a gift? Many of us give gifts of money in the name of Christ at Christmas, and find great satisfaction in giving this "gold" in honor of the Christ Child to be used for those in need rather than in the selecting of unnecessary gifts for friends.

Another gift of the Wise Men was frankincense. Why would anyone give a tiny child perfume, we may ask?

Frankincense, one of the most valuable of commodities of that time, was a most appropriate gift for *this* Child. This expensive fragrance was often associated with the idea of holiness; it was one of the chief ingredients of the holy anointing oil used for purification in the Temple, a combination of spices forbidden to ordinary persons.

Frankincense was placed on the showbread which was kept in the holiest part of the Temple, just before the bread was burned each week. It was used with the meal or sweet savour offering as part of the Hebrew worship. So, frankincense reminds us of the New Testament words about the lives of Christians having a sweet savour of life unto life.

Frankincense is a gum from a tree which grows in the Himalayas in India and also in northern Arabia, where the Wise Men originated. It is a handsome tree with clear green leaves, rather like the mountain ash, bearing pretty star-shaped pink flowers with pale yellow centers. The wood is heavy, hard and durable, and is tapped during the month of February. The Arabs cut into the bark of the tree, peeling off a thin layer. A month or so later the process is repeated and the sap flows out. When hardened by the air this resin becomes brittle, glittering and bitter to the taste. Frankincense is recognized as the finest burning resin in the world—the very word means "free-lighting."

What have we to give the Infant Saviour besides our gold? Are our lives fragrant with His presence? Do we have that happy sort of personality which brightens a gathering—or could we develop it? Perhaps that free-lighting enthusiasm, that sense of humor, that darting wit needs to be given to Him to help make others happy.

The third gift of the Wise Men was myrrh. Looking at history we see that the search for spices has occasioned many important journeys. America would not have been discovered until later had there not been a need to get the spices from India that were so important to Europeans of Columbus' time. The ancient caravan trails of the East were worn down from earliest times by the camels and donkeys of spice traders. In a day when trade between nations was limited, some of the wealthiest men were the buyers and sellers of spices and perfumery. Possibly the Wise Men themselves were traders, for they knew enough about the trade routes to return to their home "by another way."

The Bible first mentions spice traders in the story of Joseph, favorite son of Jacob. The boy's older brothers had thrown him into a pit to die, when they suddenly had a second idea—selling him to the caravan of Ishmaelites they saw coming across the dusty plain. The account tells us that the Ishmaelites were bearing spicery and balm and myrrh to Egypt, where they were sure of a sale in that luxury-loving land. The myrrh produced in their country was the sweet-smelling gum of the rock rose, a low bush that grows freely on the rocky mountainsides.

Even today people gather the gum from the plant, using soft cloth wound on a stick. The gum is rolled into balls and pressed into cakes for perfume. This is the Hebrew "lot," and is probably mistranslated "myrrh." The true myrrh comes from a very thorny bush or small tree with a large trunk and paper-thin outer bark which grew along the coast of the Red Sea as well as in southern Arabia in Bible times. When pierced, the bark emits a thick, fragrant white gum which hardens and turns reddish on exposure to air.

Myrrh, the third gift of the Wise Men, was an ingredient of the anointing oil and is often mentioned along with frankincense, as in the Song of Solomon ("I will get me to the mountain of myrrh and the hill of frankincense"). Probably these were the two most precious spices of the time and the singer of Canticles was trying to express himself in superlative language as lovers are wont to do. Or he may have referred to a hillside arboretum planted with these fragrant trees.

Myrrh was often used in the preparation of bodies for burial. Nicodemus and the women brought myrrh and other spices to wrap with the body of Jesus after His crucifixion. He had refused the myrrh mixed with wine which was offered as a sedative when He was on the cross because He wanted to stay conscious. But when His body was taken down and put into Joseph's tomb, there were the same precious fragrances that had been so respectfully presented to Him as a child by the wealthy astrologers from the East. Poor as He was all His days—"the Son of Man hath no place to lay His head"—Jesus received gifts from the rich at the beginning and end of His life.

In spite of its lovely fragrance and its great use as a perfume, somehow we usually think of the use of myrrh in embalming, and associate it only with death. How can we bring this gift to the King? Are there things in our lives that have the touch of death—the failures we continue to grieve over, the broken friendships, the sense of futility? These, too, we can bring to the manger—and there see them transformed into something that will carry fragrance into our lives and the lives of those around us.

"And when they had opened their treasures, they presented unto Him gifts, gold, frankincense and myrrh" (*Matthew* 2:11). These men were called wise. How can we be wise and give Him any less? Because they recognized the Baby as a king they brought the very best they had in their possession. To such a One we, too, should give the best we have, our energy, our ability, our time, our life.

"When they had heard the king, they departed; and, lo, the star, which they saw in the east, went before them, till it came and stood over where the young child was.

When they saw the star, they rejoiced with exceeding great joy.

And when they were come into the house, they saw the young child with Mary his mother, and fell down, and worshipped him: and when they had opened their treasures, they presented unto him gifts; gold, and frankincense, and myrrh."

—MATTHEW 2: 9-11

OUR JOURNEY TO CHRISTMAS—THROUGH ITS TWELVE days to Epiphany—is complete. But actually, it has just begun. "The gift of God is eternal life through Jesus Christ, our Lord." This is life with no beginning and no end, which has always existed in God and into which we step when we accept His gift. The message of Christmas is that God has come into our life to share it that we might share His.

"Though He was rich, yet for your sakes He became poor, that ye through His poverty might be rich."

Great are the gifts of Christmas!

"Glory to God in the Highest, and on earth peace, good will toward men."

About the author . . .

THE DAUGHTER OF MISSIONARIES, RACHEL HARTMAN was born in Hunan Province, China, and spent her first six years in that country. She then came to America by way of Europe—"which I saw," she says, "mainly astride my father's shoulders"—and began her education here.

Her literary career was launched at the age of twelve when Miss Hartman made her first sale to a magazine; it was a Christmas poem, and for it she received a check for twenty-five cents. This success led her, at junior high school, to sign autograph books with either "poetess" or "authoress" after her name.

Her interest in writing continued throughout her college years (spent at Columbia Bible College, Heidelberg College, and then at Wheaton College, where she received her A.B.), and Miss Hartman later joined *Christian Herald* magazine. She now serves as Assistant Executive Editor of that popular monthly publication.

Date Due
